CONTENTS

Photo © Richard Day

ABOUT JOE AND MARY ANN MCDONALD

Joe and Mary Ann McDonald are professional wildlife photographers with a special interest in Polar Bears and Big Cats. Joe is the author of eleven books on wildlife or wildlife photography, and Mary Ann is the author of twenty-nine children's books.

Joe and Mary spend over half the year in the field photographing, leading photo safaris, and conducting tours to worldwide destinations that typically include five continents. They currently reside in McClure, PA. Learn more at www.hoothollow.com.

Top—The author, Joe McDonald, on a Zodiac in Svalbard, patiently waiting for some Atlantic Walruses to wake up.

Bottom—Joe and Mary Ann McDonald have made numerous trips to the Arctic, for Polar Bears and other wildlife. They lead photo tours to Svalbard and to more temperate areas around the globe.

ACKNOWLEDGMENTS

As a photographer and writer, I was faced with the sobering reality that my wife, Mary Ann, and I simply did not have the diversity of Polar Bear photographs to adequately tell this bear's wonderful story. Fortunately, we have friends who are talented amateur photographers, ecotourist guides, and professional photographers who, like us, lead tours to Polar Bear country. All were happy to help, and their contributions to this book were invaluable and helped to make this one of the most diverse collections of Polar Bear photographs ever published.

I must thank my two great friends, Tom Wester and Steve Metildi, who immediately came on board and offered their images,

POLAR BEARS
in the WILD

A Visual Essay of an Endangered Species

WITHDRAWN

JOE MCDONALD
Amherst Media, Inc. ■ Buffalo, NY

Published by:
Amherst Media, Inc.
PO BOX 538
Buffalo, NY 14213
www.AmherstMedia.com

Publisher: Craig Alesse
Senior Editor/Production Manager: Michelle Perkins
Editors: Barbara A. Lynch-Johnt, Beth Alesse
Acquisitions Editor: Harvey Goldstein
Associate Publisher: Katie Kiss
Editorial Assistance from: Carey A. Miller, Roy Bakos, Jen Sexton-Riley, Rebecca Rudell
Business Manager: Sarah Loder
Marketing Associate: Tonya Flickinger

ISBN-13: 978-1-68203-336-4
Library of Congress Control Number: 2017963170
Printed in the United States of America
10 9 8 7 6 5 4 3 2 1

AUTHOR A BOOK WITH AMHERST MEDIA!

Are you an accomplished photographer with devoted fans? Consider authoring a book with us and share your quality images and wisdom with your fans. It's a great way to build your business and brand through a high-quality, full-color printed book sold worldwide. Our experienced team makes it easy and rewarding for each book sold—no cost to you. E-mail **submissions@amherstmedia.com** today!

www.facebook.com/AmherstMediaInc
www.youtube.com/AmherstMedia
www.twitter.com/AmherstMedia

which include Tom's Kermode Bear, a bear I've not seen in the wild, and Steve's diverse images from Churchill.

Katherine Pierce's credit, Katherine Pierce/CureUs Designs, tells it all, as profits from the sales of her images are donated to the American Cancer Society. On one of our photo tours, Kathy showed a few of her incredible mom-and-cub photos from Wapsuk National Park, and I'm glad I remembered her doing so. She's spent more time there than anyone else I know and has the images to prove it!

My friend and our expedition leader for our Svalbard Polar Bear trips, Adam Rheborg, has been leading ecotourists and photographers to Svalbard and other Arctic destinations for over twenty years. As a guide, his focus is on his people, not his photography, but nevertheless, Adam has amassed an incredible collection of images, depicting behavior I'm still dying to see.

Years ago, Mary and I met a Denali guide and photographer, Hugh Rose, who later started his own company and now leads photo tours to the northern coast of Alaska and elsewhere. When I thought about getting complete coverage, I thought of Hugh, for his shots of bears on whales and his low-light, ground-level shots. Hugh's incredible images of bears from this less well-known photography destination are superb.

Richard Day, a good friend and fellow photo tour leader, supplied more images from Churchill. Richard led photo tours to Churchill for over a decade and has perhaps the best coverage of Churchill's bears and wildlife.

I was also very fortunate to have two other good friends, Sue Altenburg and Ivan Rothman, show portfolios on one of our tours that included their Polar Bears photos. Had that not happened, I'd have missed some great images included here.

Although I relied on a diverse number of books and resources in writing this book, I must thank Morten Jørgensen for really opening my eyes to the hunting and research issues involved with Polar Bear management in the far north. I'd strongly recommend Morten's book, *Polar Bears on the Edge* (NHBS, 2015), for anyone concerned about bears, and their potential mismanagement.

I'd also like to thank Joe Johnson and his staff at Really Right Stuff, Clay Wimberley from Wimberley Tripod Heads, Lou Schmidt from Hoodman, and Chris Breeze from BreezeBrowser for all their help and support.

Last but certainly not least, I have to give the most credit to my wife, Mary Ann, who does most of the work in putting our photo tours together, does the tours and photographs, too, and helped me put together this book.

WEBSITES

hughrosephotography.com

daybreakimagery.photoshelter.com

cureusdesigns.com

stevemetildi.com

reallyrightstuff.com

tripodhead.com

breezebrowser.com

hoothollow.com

polar-quest.com

INTRODUCTION

Standing on the deck of the small ship, the *M/S Stockholm*, I scanned a landscape of frightening monotony, a crumpled blanket of snow and ice extending left and right and onto the horizon, under a canopy of a brilliant blue and cloudless sky. No living thing was in sight, no bird flew overhead, no dark, comma-shaped dots signifying the presence of a hauled-out seal, nothing but the cold, corrugated surface of unending ice fields. How could anything live in this landscape, let alone the largest terrestrial predator on earth? Experiencing the environment of the ice bear, the Polar Bear, first hand, infused in me an even greater appreciation for this magnificent predator, this, the king of the Arctic landscape.

Polar Bears are one of the most recognized and well-known animals in the entire world. And yet, despite its fame and familiarity, the Polar Bear lives in one of the most remote and infrequently visited locations on our planet, the Arctic. This is the land of snow and ice, and the Polar Bear is the apex predator of this habitat, but these great white bears are also found far south of the Arctic Circle. On the southern shores of Canada's James Bay at the same latitude as London, England, Polar Bears spend the summer on land, waiting for the cold of winter and the ice they need for hunting.

The Polar Bear is also considered a marine mammal, which might seem odd considering its cousins, the six other species of bear (the North American Black Bear, Asiatic Black Bear, Brown Bear or Grizzly, Spectacled Bear, Sloth Bear, and Sun Bear) are all terrestrial, land-based mammals. As a marine mammal, Polar Bears share that rather loose grouping with walruses, seals, whales, and sea otters, all mammals closely associated with a life in the sea. A Polar Bear, however, may spend its entire life in or on water, as ice is just the solid form of water. A Polar Bear cub born in an ice cave in a sheltered ridge of pack ice could spend the rest of its life walking the ice, stalking seals and seeking carrion, or swimming from one ice floe to another.

The bear, as a predator, must of course feed on other forms of life, and despite one's first impressions of this as a cold and barren land, the Arctic is the home to a variety of life, including some of the largest bird colonies on earth. Dovekies, or Little Auks, nest in some areas by the multiple hundreds of thousands, and Black-legged Kittiwakes, a graceful species of gull, carpet sea cliffs in what seems to be uncountable numbers. To stand at the base of one of these colonies, enveloped by the sounds of thousands of screeching birds swirling in the sky above, is an unforgettable experience, but one best done with your mouth clamped shut. In the

Arctic seas, Ringed Seals, the Polar Bear's favorite prey, number well over two million, making it one of the most numerous of all mammal species, followed by huge numbers of Harp and Bearded Seals. You will be introduced to many of these animals, many important to the Polar Bear, and all a vital part of the Arctic ecosystem.

The Arctic is a remote and sparsely inhabited land by man, and travel, research, and census-taking is limited and dangerous, especially for those studying the Polar Bear. Accordingly, knowing the exact number of any species in this region, particularly the Polar Bear, is impossible, and can only be estimated or guessed. Exactly how many Polar Bears roam the Arctic wilderness is unknown, and estimates range from a high of approximately 25,000 to a low of 16,000, a frightening discrepancy of over 40 percent. Yet since the 1960s, when the threat of extinction for the Polar Bear was finally recognized and some protections were enacted, perhaps 40,000 Polar Bears have been killed, a number that is quite likely twice the number of bears presently alive. How and why these wide-ranging estimates pose grave danger to the bear will be explored later in this book.

Today, this magnificent predator, the largest non-marine carnivore on Earth, is in danger of extinction. When I began this book I, like too many, was only vaguely aware of the threats facing the Arctic regions and the Polar Bear. As our Earth warms, the Arctic is doing so at nearly twice the speed of the rest of the planet. Ice melts earlier in the spring and freezes later in the fall. Pack ice retreats, stranding Polar Bears

on barren land where food is scarce. With more open water, stronger storms and higher waves develop, breaking up ice that was once fairly secure, increasing the amount of open ocean and setting the stage for even greater wave action and further ice erosion and breakup. Since the range of the Polar Bear is defined by the extent of winter sea ice, its very existence is dependent upon ice. In many areas, that critical ice is vanishing, literally melting beneath the Polar Bear's huge paws.

One could, perhaps, liken the Polar Bear to the proverbial canary in the coal mine, a harbinger of threats all of us may face in the not too distant future. In that way, the bear is playing a critical role, becoming an icon for the threat of global warming. Of course, the Polar Bear holds such fascination for so many other reasons. Its color is unique, ranging from a nearly pigment-free pure white to a dirty yellow, and even brownish-black if this white bear has spent much time on land. It is a big, imposing animal as well, with males often over 1,000 pounds. And as a predator, the bear evokes a special, visceral mystique for a variety of reasons. Perhaps though, it is the land itself, so remote and seemingly so hostile, cold and dark and barren, and our knowing that the Polar Bear thrives in an environment so challenging to us that it makes this predator such a precious inhabitant of the world we share. This book will showcase much of what makes this bear one of the world's favorite animals.

MEET THE BEAR

At least 150,000 years ago, and perhaps three times farther back in time, the ancestor of today's Polar Bear wandered the far north, tentatively stepping onto the ice to scavenge or to hunt for seals. Over time, adaptations that enhanced a bear's survival in this foreign landscape occurred, and with time, a new bear arose from the old, the bear we now call the Polar Bear. That ancestor was the Brown or Grizzly Bear, and even today on the northern coast of Alaska and the far northern reaches of this bear's range in Canada, Grizzly Bears occasionally move onto the ice, either to scavenge from kills or to hunt for seals.

Unlike its omnivorous ancestor, eating both plant and animal life, Polar Bears became consummate carnivores; in fact,

the largest of all terrestrial predators. These adaptations have exquisitely fine-tuned the Polar Bear for a life on the ice and on the sea.

FAMILIARITY (PREVIOUS PAGE)
The Polar Bear is one of the best-known animals on the planet. School children around the world instantly recognize this unique mammal, the great white bear of the far north.

COMICAL & CUTE (TOP)
Photo: Hugh Rose/hughrose photography.com
Because of a Polar Bear's habit of drying and cleaning its fur on snow, the bear often adopts poses and postures we can identify with. Watching a wild Polar Bear can make you laugh, and certainly smile, as the bear wiggles and rolls upon the snow.

PERFECT HABITAT (BOTTOM)
Polar Bears are denizens of the ice, and their survival depends upon ice, as this is where these bears hunt for their favorite prey, seals. Pack ice moves with the wind and ocean currents, traveling great distances in doing so. Despite this, bears maintain a fidelity to a particular range, even while the world literally passes beneath their feet.

BUILT FOR THE SNOW

(PREVIOUS PAGE, TOP)

Polar Bears have long, nearly serpentine necks, giving the bear an advantage when it crashes into a Ringed Seal's lair. The tapered shape allows the bear's head and neck to slip easily and quickly into the seal's den and, if the bear is lucky, to catch a seal before it can dash into the sea.

A VARIETY OF SHADES

(PREVIOUS PAGE, BOTTOM)

Asked to describe a Polar Bear's color, one would invariably answer, "It's white." In truth, most bears have a yellowish tint to their fur. On Svalbard ships, Arctic tourism guides scan the ice for yellow-tinted shapes, as these may prove to be bears.

A TAPERED HEAD (TOP)

Photo: Steve Metildi

The head of a Polar Bear is long and some-what pointed, giving it a more streamlined appearance than the dish-shaped head and face of its closest relative, the Grizzly Bear. The long snout helps in warming air as the bear draws in each breath in the arctic cold.

PUTTING ON THE POUNDS (BOTTOM)

Photo: Hugh Rose/hughrosephotography.com

While obesity is often detrimental to our health, in Polar Bears, a thick layer of fat is important for survival. Bears will live off this stored fat during the lean times of the year.

STRANDED (TOP)

Photo: Tom Wester

In many parts of the Polar Bear's summer range, bears go hungry when the snow and ice disappear, as seals spend their time at sea, leaving the bears with little or nothing to eat. During the warmer months, Polar Bears may go without food for weeks on end until the ice returns and the bears can begin again to hunt for seals.

A GOOD MOTHER (BOTTOM)

Photo: Katherine Pierce/CureUs Designs

Pregnant Polar Bears may fast, eating nothing at all from the time the last ice melts, in July, until they emerge from their dens in March or April with their newborn cubs. A mother bear may lose half her body weight during that time. To survive and to nourish newborn young, females must pile on fat while the ice remains and seals are available.

FORMIDABLE JAWS (TOP LEFT)

Photo: Adam Rheborg

A Polar Bear's diet is almost exclusively meat, and their skull and dentition reflects this. Polar Bears have the largest canines of any bear, although in male bears these long fangs are often broken down to mere stubs, as the males clash to establish dominance or possession of a female in estrous.

THE BEAR'S TAIL (TOP RIGHT)

Photo: Katherine Pierce/CureUs Designs

Like all bears, a Polar Bear has a very short tail that has little functionality. From this angle, a Polar Bear's sex can usually be determined, as the fur beneath the tail of a female is often stained a yellowish-brown from urine. This bear is likely a male.

IT'S A GIRL! (BOTTOM)

Photo: Adam Rheborg

The dark stain on this bear's rump is a clear indication that this bear is a female. A Polar Bear's skin is actually black, and appears to be visible in this image along the insides of her thighs.

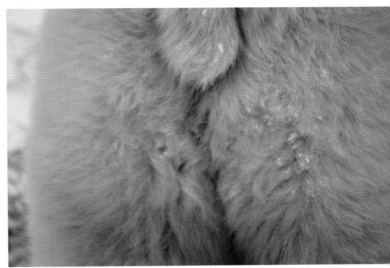

MISTAKEN IDENTITY (TOP)

Seen from behind, the sun-bleached fur of this Grizzly Bear in Denali National Park appears white, and is as pale as the fur of many Polar Bears. Barren-ground Grizzlies, as this population is sometimes called, can be very light colored, while the same species, along the Alaskan coast, can be nearly black.

SEPARATE POPULATIONS (BOTTOM)

While all Polar Bears look fairly similar and could theoretically, roam anywhere across the Arctic, scientists have divided the bears into nineteen separate populations. Most of the bears in each population remain within a specific area. Because of this, Polar Bears have been subjected to varying levels of hunting based on assumed population numbers, numbers that are often based on outdated guesstimates.

BEAR FEET (TOP)

In contrast to other bears, the bottom of a Polar Bear's foot is thickly furred, with only a limited area of exposed skin. Although the bare pads of the feet may look smooth, this skin is covered with tiny papillae, analogous to the Velcro-like pads of a Gecko lizard. This gives the bear traction on smooth ice, aided of course by the bear's short and very sharp claws.

SHARP CLAWS (BOTTOM)

Photo: Adam Rheborg

Although the Polar Bear is closely related to the Grizzly, the Polar Bear's claws more closely resemble those of the Black Bear.

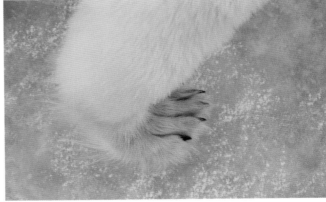

Both of those bears have claws that are relatively short and also very sharp. These sharp claws enable a Black Bear to climb trees and assist the Polar Bear in snagging slippery seals.

BEAR TRACKS (TOP)

Photo: Tom Wester

Distinct toe pads and claw marks are clearly evident in this Polar Bear track. Bears walk flat-footed, described as a plantigrade step, with heels and toes pressing to the ice or earth just as our feet do. Most four-footed mammals walk either on their toes or on the very tip of the toes.

LONG CLAWS (BOTTOM)

Alaskan Brown Bears, the coastal form of the Grizzly, have extremely long claws, as seen here. While Polar Bears are almost exclusively meat-eaters, or carnivores, a Grizzly Bear is an omnivore, and its diet includes both plants and animals. The Grizzly's long claws assist in digging, both to root up plants or to dig out ground squirrels and, along coastal rivers, the claws help the bear to pin down or swat sleek salmon.

FAT FOR A REASON (TOP)

Photo: Adam Rheborg

Polar Bears are the largest land carnivore, and fat adult males may weigh over 1,700 pounds. When the hunting is good, a bear may catch a seal every three to five days, and in doing so eat only the seal's calorie-rich blubber. Polar Bears convert over 97 percent of a seal's blubber to their own fat, vital for sustaining the bears when the ice melts and bears return to land, when they're likely to lose between 25 and 50 percent of their body weight before the ice returns and seal hunting resumes.

A BROWN POLAR BEAR (BOTTOM)

Photo: Adam Rheborg

This Polar Bear is as dark as many Grizzly or Brown Bears, but his dark color is only a temporary condition. The fur of bears marooned on land throughout the summer may become stained or dirty, even though Polar Bears are remarkably fastidious in their cleanliness. It is typical for a Polar Bear to take breaks while feeding to wash blood or grease from its fur.

A WHITE BEAR (TOP)

Photo: Katherine Pierce/CureUs Designs
Young Polar Bear cubs are nearly pure white, but older bears typically have a duller coloration. This adult bear's bright-white fur is unusual, but would no doubt assist in hiding the bear on white snow or ice when it is hunting seals.

REFLECTING COLOR (CENTER AND BOTTOM)

Photos: Richard Day
The time of day and the conditions of the sky can alter the outward appearance of a Polar Bear, tinting its fur in various shades of color. Waiting for freeze-up on the tundra in Churchill, Manitoba, Polar Bears may even glow orange, their fur reflecting the last rays of sunlight before the Arctic night.

NORTHERN PREDATOR (TOP)

Photo: Katherine Pierce/CureUs Designs

Most people, I assume, know that Polar Bears only inhabit the Northern Hemisphere, the Arctic regions. While Polar Bears could survive, and perhaps thrive, in Antarctica, climate and vast geographic obstacles prevented Polar Bears from migrating there. At times, some misguided souls have entertained the idea of introducing Polar Bears to that continent for various reasons, ranging from conserving the species to providing sport for hunters. Fortunately, this has never happened.

ALLEN'S RULE (CENTER)

Photo: Steve Metildi

In 1877, zoologist Joel Asaph Allen made the observation that animals living in cold climates have smaller appendages, including limbs and ears, than animals living in warm climates. This is clearly evident in the ears of the Polar Bear, although this species still has fairly long and very powerful legs.

BLACK BEARS (BOTTOM)

Black Bears in southern Arizona's mountains live in a hot environment, and the larger ears of this population are clearly visible. In desert regions, bears are thinner than their Arctic cousin, who needs a larger body mass to retain heat.

PEAR SHAPED (TOP)

Photo: Hugh Rose/hughrosephotography.com

Polar Bears are built for the cold, with smaller ears, longer snouts, thick and round bodies, and powerful mid-sized legs. In the low light of a polar afternoon, this bear practically glows, reflecting the sunlight off its clean, white fur. At one time, it was thought that a bear's fur conducted light like fiber optics down to the skin, but this has proven to be false. Still, the fur alone provides wonderful insulation.

KERMODE/"SPIRIT" BEAR (BOTTOM)

Photo: Tom Wester

The American Black Bear has several color variations, including a bluish phase, called the Glacier Bear; a cinnamon phase, most common in the American Rockies; and a nearly white phase, often called "the Spirit Bear," that superficially resembles a Polar Bear. The Kermode Bear's white color may aid the bear in catching salmon during the day in its rainforest habitat in coastal western Canada.

EVOLUTION (TOP)

Polar Bears evolved from the Brown, or Grizzly Bear, somewhere around 100,000 to 150,000 years ago or earlier. This separation is still so new that the two species can interbreed and produce fertile young, which has occurred in zoos on multiple occasions. In 2006, the first wild Grizzly-Polar Bear hybrid was encountered, shot by a Polar Bear hunter. Since that date, other hybrids have been found, including one that was a second-generation cross.

SHORELINE SCAVENGERS

(BOTTOM LEFT AND RIGHT)

The omnivorous Brown Bear, or Grizzly, may find enough to eat as it hunts tidal flats and meadows, whereas shore leave is a time of fasting for the Polar Bear. Hungry Polar Bears may eat kelp or algae washed ashore but derive little nutritive value from these meager meals.

ICE HUNTER (RIGHT)

The Polar Bear is superbly adapted for a life on the ice, and as soon as the sea or ocean water freezes, bears vanish from the land. Some Polar Bears may remain on the ice their entire life, moving north with the pack ice as the ice retreats during the warmer months, and following the ice edge south as winter advances.

THE POLAR BEAR'S WORLD

The Polar Bear's world is one of cold and ice, with temperatures that may drop below -50 degrees Fahrenheit in winter, under skies that may pulsate magically with displays of the northern lights. In winter, for bears living high above the Arctic Circle, their world may be one of perpetual gloom, dimly lit by the stars and moon and by the faint glow along the southern horizon from a land where the sun still shines.

Ice is the key to the Polar Bear's world. This is a challenging landscape where few humans have learned to live, but one where the adaptations of the Polar Bear have allowed it to thrive, at least until relatively recently. The Polar Bear's thick fur coat insulates it from the cold, and the bear's ability to swim long distances in frigid seas enables the Polar Bear to reach land or pack ice, or to hunt from ice floe to floe for resting seals.

ON THE EDGE (BELOW)

Photo: Tom Wester

Standing on a platform of rocks iced in hoar frost and snow, a male Polar Bear peers out toward Hudson Bay, waiting for freeze-up and perhaps his first meal in at least three months.

NIGHT FALLS AND HUNTING BEGINS (FOLLOWING PAGE)

Photo: Hugh Rose/hughrosephotography.com

In some portions of the Polar Bear's range, when the sun sets, darkness remains for weeks or months. Temperatures plummet, but seal hunting actually is easier at this time than during the summer months, when much of the ice melts. During this long polar night, Polar Bears hunt the ice for seals that are often restricted to a series of breathing holes and are not free to roam.

LAND OF PERPETUAL NIGHT (TOP)

Photo: Tom Wester

The Arctic is often called the Land of the Midnight Sun, and indeed in summer, the sun may not set for several weeks. Conversely, the highest latitudes of the Arctic could be called the Land of Perpetual Night, as the sun never rises above the horizon during winter. On polar nights, however, the moon, stars, and refracted sunlight on the distant southern horizon provide some light, allowing Polar Bears to remain active in this land of darkness.

THE NORTHERN LIGHTS (CENTER)

Photo: Katherine Pierce/CureUs Designs

During the Arctic night, the sky may shimmer with ethereal colors, ribbons of light that dance across the sky. This is the aurora borealis, the northern lights, a phenomenon triggered by the solar wind, where charged particles from the sun collide with gas molecules in the upper reaches of Earth's atmosphere. One wonders if the Polar Bear appreciates these spectacles.

CONGREGATIONS (BOTTOM)

Photo: Hugh Rose/hughrosephotography.com

Along the coast of northern Alaska, Polar Bears may gather in surprising numbers. Polar Bears are normally thought of as solitary animals, but as winter nears and bears move to the coasts awaiting freeze-up, large numbers can be seen together. Surprisingly, the bears often interact, with cubs playing or young males wrestling as they await the cold.

FREEZE-UP (TOP)

Photo: Steve Metildi

During the summer in Churchill, Manitoba, Polar Bears are marooned on land for months. With the arrival of winter and cold weather, Hudson Bay may freeze in just a few days. When it does, virtually every bear disappears, as all head out to the ice and for their first meal in months.

FAST ICE (BOTTOM)

Some of the best hunting occurs on the "fast ice," named because the ice is attached to the land or glaciers and is held "fast" or stable. Ringed Seals, the Polar Bear's favorite food, maintain breathing holes in the fast ice, providing sure locations for bears to hunt, as they wait for a seal to appear.

PACK ICE (TOP)

Polar Bears regularly patrol the floating pack ice, where Bearded Seals often haul out for a rest or a sleep. Pack ice floats with the wind and the ocean currents, and enormous but disjointed sheets of ice may drift for hundreds of miles. Still, in this transient landscape, Polar Bears maintain home ranges, and will return to the same region year after year despite the drifting that may occur.

BREAK UP (BOTTOM LEFT AND RIGHT)

Photos: Adam Rheborg

As summer advances, the fast ice begins to melt, sometimes breaking off into large sheets that may, eventually, drift far from land and become a part of the pack ice. As global temperatures rise and ice cover declines, greater and greater areas of open water result. Bears, hunting the pack ice, often have to swim great distances from one ice floe to another.

ICE FLOES (TOP)

A landscape with equal amounts of open water and ice floes provides ample habitat for Polar Bears, as Bearded Seals are common in this landscape. While this Polar Bear appears to be sleeping, appearances are deceiving. Should a seal surface nearby, the bear will begin a hunt.

ON THE EDGE (CENTER)

When the fast ice begins to break up, Polar Bears have two areas for pursuing seals. Closer to shore, where the ice is still solid, Ringed Seals maintain their breathing holes in the ice, while at the interface of ice and sea, seals may haul out to rest or to sleep. In either case, the most productive hunting is over the continental shelf where the sea is the shallowest and access to food greatest for the seals.

BROKEN GLASS (BOTTOM)

Photo: Adam Rheborg

A Polar Bear negotiates a route across shards of ice that remind one of a broken window pane. The Velcro-like pads and sharp claws of the Polar Bear's feet assist in traction as the bear walks across what, to us humans, would be an impossible landscape to negotiate.

DRIFTING (TOP)

Since pack ice moves with
the ocean currents and
wind, a Polar Bear may
travel hundreds of miles
from its original location.
Maintaining a home range,
Polar Bears will eventually
return to the approximate
location where they be-
gan their journey. While
there are many theories, no
one really knows how the
bears navigate through a
landscape often devoid of
landmarks.

STAYING DRY (BOTTOM)

Photo: Adam Rheborg
While Polar Bears are
accomplished swimmers,
bears often avoid getting
wet by jumping small gaps
or taking a circuitous route.
Mothers with cubs are
especially prone to avoid
water, as cubs, with their
smaller total body mass,
could suffer hypothermia
in the ice-cold water. When
swimming cannot be avoid-
ed, small cubs often ride on
their mother's back to stay
partially dry.

COLLAPSE (TOP)

Each year, the fast ice melts earlier in the spring, and travel across the ice becomes more difficult as the ice thins. Bears will splay themselves like a starfish to disperse their weight when crossing thin ice, although sometimes they still crash through. Repeated dunks and the effort to climb back onto the ice burns up valuable energy the bears will need during the lean months of late summer and fall.

FAMILY SWIM (CENTER)

Photo: Hugh Rose/hughrosephotography.com
When necessary, Polar Bears can swim long distances, nearly 100 miles in some cases. The Arctic seas are often calm, but storms can arise, generating waves that make any long swim arduous and dangerous. While an adult bear may survive a long swim, or one in turbulent waters, cubs probably will not. As the polar ice shrinks, storms and waves are expected to increase, and with it, one could expect Polar Bear numbers to suffer.

DUNKING FOR SEALS (BOTTOM)

We watched this Polar Bear for hours as it dug into the snow and ice, sometimes dipping into open water or diving in and swimming underwater for several yards before resurfacing. Such efforts expend a lot of energy, and although the bear didn't look thin, we wondered if it was indeed hungry and this prompted its behavior.

PROTECTED SPECIES (ABOVE)

The Polar Bear is protected in the U.S. under the Marine Mammal Act, and one can understand why it is considered a marine mammal after watching a bear swim and dive through the cold Arctic seas. Bears generally hold their breath for less than one minute, still quite a feat in 30-degree water that would literally take the breath away from a swimming human!

THE BIG SHAKE (FOLLOWING PAGE, TOP LEFT)

Like a shaggy dog, a Polar Bear gives a vigorous shake that ripples down its body, spewing water everywhere in the first step in drying off.

BACK RUB (FOLLOWING PAGE, TOP RIGHT)

Polar Bears are fastidious in their cleanliness, and scientists who tranquilize and tag these white bears report they are nearly odorless. Clean fur is essential to maintain the loft in their fur for the insulation necessary in a climate that can drop to -50 degrees Fahrenheit.

BELLY RUB (FOLLOWING PAGE, BOTTOM)

Snow acts as a great drying agent, and a Polar Bear will slide along on its belly, propelled by the claws of its hind legs, sometimes traveling a dozen yards or more before rolling to its side or back and rubbing itself dry.

SNOW CAKES (TOP)

Photo: Hugh Rose/hughrosephotography.com
Snow clings in bunches to the wet fur of a Polar Bear, acting as a drying agent as soon as the bear shakes. These shakes and rolls are always comical to watch and provide tourists and photographers wonderful opportunities for funny poses.

FLYING SNOW (BOTTOM)

Photo: Katherine Pierce/CureUs Designs
A Polar Bear awakes after a snowfall, shaking himself dry. Snow is actually a good source of insulation, and pregnant Polar Bears sometimes den on open slopes where accumulating snow will eventually create the foundations for her den.

SNOW MOUND OR BEAR? (TOP)

Photo: Adam Rheborg

A sleeping bear, covered by fresh snow, is indistinguishable from other snow mounds; a frustrating fact for tourist guides intent on spotting bears! Bears marooned on land may spend most of their time sleeping, and even those hunting the pack ice may sleep for hours or days, snugly curled in a furry ball.

LEAN TIMES (BOTTOM)

Once the fast ice melts, Polar Bears either move onto the pack ice, if it is within range of a long walk or swim, or remain land-locked where meals are meager, few, and far between. The next substantial meal may not occur for four months or longer, when winter returns and, with it, the ice.

" THIS FAT BEAR, STRANDED ON AN ALASKAN BEACH

UNTIL THE WINTER SEA ICE RETURNS, IS LIKELY TO LOSE

AT LEAST A THIRD OF ITS BODY WEIGHT BY THEN."

WIDE BODY (BELOW)

Photo: Hugh Rose/hughrosephotography.com
Luckily, Polar Bears don't travel in commercial jets, as this bear's huge girth would overflow any seat! This fat bear, stranded on an Alaskan beach until the winter sea ice returns, is likely to lose at least a third of its body weight by then.

DANGEROUS TIMES <small>(ABOVE)</small>

Photo: Hugh Rose/hughrosephotography.com

Thin bears, marooned on land for several months, may face starvation. This is especially true for cubs that lack the mass of a much larger bear. During these lean months, Polar Bears will go into what is termed "walking hibernation," as their metabolism slows and conserves energy, but without requiring the bear to go into a deep sleep. Bears can enter or exit this state as food availability changes.

> **THIN BEARS, MAROONED ON LAND FOR SEVERAL MONTHS, MAY FACE STARVATION."**

ON THE LAND

Though the Arctic landscape may seem barren and bleak, it is rich with life, and in some areas abundantly so. In late spring, Snow Geese colonies can carpet the tundra by the hundreds of thousands, and along sea cliffs Murres and Kittiwakes blanket every available ledge, crowding so close together that only the gap between the outstretched neck of one bird separates it from the next. For the Polar Bear, however, the time spent on land can be one of hardship, for despite the abundance of birds, most are unobtainable or provide so few calories that the effort involved is too costly compared to the return.

In areas like Churchill, Manitoba, Canada, Polar Bears may find themselves marooned on Hudson Bay's southern shore for eight months of the year. Here, bears spend these warm months in a tundra landscape dotted with willows and spruce trees, sharing the land with foxes, wolves, caribou, and a variety of birds.

The wildlife of the tundra, seashore, and cliffs is intriguing, if ephemeral. The countless birds lining the cliffs in spring and early summer vanish by mid-summer, returning to the sea, where they spend most of their lives. Food is scarce for the Polar Bear, relieved at times only by the discovery of a dead whale or walrus that washes ashore, or an injured caribou that stumbles into the bear's path. Hungry Polar Bears, particularly subadults that have not yet mastered their hunting skills, may get into trouble when they wander into a village or settlement looking for food. For the Polar Bear, winter cannot come too quickly.

SAXIFRAGE (BELOW)

In terms of actual rainfall, the high Arctic is considered a desert, as the region typically receives less than 10 inches of precipitation a year. The landscape is treeless, and most plants hug the earth. Saxifrage is one such plant.

HUNGRY & HUNTING (TOP LEFT)

Photo: Tom Wester

In Churchill, Manitoba, the prevailing winds push Hudson Bay's pack ice to the south, where it eventually melts, stranding Polar Bears along its southern shores. Some bears stay put, waiting for winter's ice, but most begin a long migration to the northwest, where ice will return first. Most find little or nothing to eat during this long walk.

SVALBARD REINDEER (TOP RIGHT)

Small herds of Svalbard Reindeer share the land with the Polar Bears that find themselves land-bound through the summer months. Although an occasional calf or a sick or injured reindeer may be taken, healthy adults of these fleet-footed members of the deer family can easily outrun a hungry bear.

A SHED HORN (BOTTOM)

Photo: Hugh Rose/hughrosephotography.com

A Polar Bear cub plays with the shed antler of a caribou on Alaska's coastal plain.

Bears will readily scavenge any reindeer or caribou carcass they find, and perhaps the lingering scent of the caribou drew this cub's attention.

SCAVENGING REINDEER (TOP)

Photo: Ivan Rothman

By pulling and tugging, two Polar Bears dismember a winter-killed caribou near Churchill, Manitoba. While not intentionally doing so, splitting carcasses in this way allows both bears to feed while lessening the chance of altercations over the meat.

CAMOUFLAGED HENS (BOTTOM LEFT)

The hens of Eider Ducks are well camouflaged, providing some protection from aerial predators. The hens pluck down from their breasts and belly feathers to line the nest, providing the most efficient form of

insulation known. Local human residents often harvest Eider down, being careful to only take a small quantity from each nest so as not to endanger the eggs.

SEEKING SAFETY (BOTTOM RIGHT)

In Svalbard, Norway, a large colony of Common Eider Ducks nest in the open ground around a sled dog kennel where barking dogs deter hungry foxes. In this photo, only the conspicuously patterned male Eiders are visible, although most are paired with a well-camouflaged hen sitting on her nest nearby.

EGG HUNTER (TOP)

A pair of canny Arctic Foxes discovered that kenneled sled dogs posed no threat, and regularly raided the Eider colony for eggs. Two or three eggs would satisfy the appetite of any eight-pound Arctic Fox, but the foxes grabbed eggs constantly throughout the nesting season, digging holes and caching the eggs for future consumption.

TURNING WHITE (BOTTOM)

Photo: Steve Metildi

As winter approaches, Arctic Foxes molt, replacing their summer gray or bluish fur with a fluffy coat of white. In winter, Arctic Foxes scavenge from the kills of Polar Bears, as Polar Bears often consume only the seal's blubber, leaving the rest of the seal untouched. Foxes will follow bears far out onto the pack ice.

ARCTIC WHITE (TOP)

Photo: Richard Day

The fluffy, thick coat of this adult Arctic Fox protects it from the winter cold. Although Arctic Foxes have been seen over 100 miles out onto the pack ice, the foxes must return to land before the ice melts. Unlike sea-going mammals like the Polar Bear or Sea Otter, the fur of the Arctic Fox will saturate, and a fox would chill and die if exposed to cold water for any length of time.

ARCTIC TERNS (BOTTOM)

The graceful Arctic Tern is famous for having the longest migration of any bird, as birds regularly migrate to the Antarctic regions and back every year. Terns are fierce defenders of their nests and chicks, and will dive-bomb lumbering bears intent upon nest raiding, although these four-ounce birds will have little effect on a 1,000 pound bear.

THE DOVEKIE (LEFT)

The Dovekie, or Little Auk, nests on rocky talus slopes in the high Arctic in the hundreds of thousands. After the nesting season, Dovekies spend the rest of their time at sea, sometimes wandering as far as southern New Jersey on the United States' Atlantic coast. Bears may, on occasion, attempt to dig or root out nesting Dovekies, but the meal doesn't justify the effort.

A DANGEROUS PERCH (RIGHT)

Photo: Adam Rheborg

High on a sea cliff, a Polar Bear attempts to raid the nests of Brünnich Guillemots. The sheer cliffs provide security for the birds, and potentially instant death for a bear that slips from these narrow, precarious ledges. The caloric benefit for such risky efforts is minimal, but still tempting, for a Polar Bear marooned on a seal-less island for several months.

// BEARS MAY, ON OCCASION, ATTEMPT TO DIG OR ROOT OUT
NESTING DOVEKIES, BUT THE MEAL DOESN'T JUSTIFY THE EFFORT."

WING TO WING (TOP)

Brünnich Guillemots nest tightly together, with some birds perched on snowbanks still covering their nest sites from previous years. Here, birds are safe from most potential predators. When the nestlings fledge, the young birds will launch themselves on still-developing wings, gliding and flapping as they attempt to reach the sea hundreds of feet below. Many fall short, crashing into the shoreline rocks where Arctic Foxes wait, grabbing every chick they can.

PATIENTLY WAITING

(BOTTOM)

Photo: Steve Metildi

In the southernmost extension of the Polar Bear's range, on the shores of James and Hudson Bays, stunted spruce trees poke into the sky. This area in Manitoba and northern Ontario is one of the few places where one can see both Polar Bears and trees, as most of the bear's range is either ice, treeless tundra, or rocky shorelines.

ARCTIC HARE (TOP)

As winter nears, Arctic Hares shed their brown summer coat to one of white. This molt is determined by the photo period, the length of daylight, and not by local weather conditions. As the climate warms and snow falls later in the season, hares and Willow Ptarmigan, a bird that also molts from brown to white, may sport a conspicuous white coat long before this camouflage plays any effective role, exposing both to predators.

A LUCKY BEAR (BOTTOM)

Photo: Steve Metildi
On the shores of Hudson Bay, a Polar Bear feeds on a seal kill. Such opportunities are quite rare before freeze-up, when the entire Bay is covered with ice and bears can target seal holes and small leads of open water where seals are likely to frequent.

A RED FOX? (TOP LEFT)

Photo: Steve Metildi

The Red Fox, Vulpes vulpes, is found across the Northern Hemisphere and demonstrates a wide range of color variations. One is the striking Silver Fox, sometimes seen around Churchill, Manitoba. Another variant is called the Cross Fox, where dark fur on the shoulders and along the back resembles a cross, at least when a fox is skinned and drying on a fur trapper's rack.

COLOR MORPH (TOP RIGHT)

Photo: Steve Metildi

The typical color morph of a Red Fox gives this fox its common name. Red Foxes may, on occasion, scavenge along the pack ice close to shore. Arctic and Red Foxes and Gray Wolves share portions of their range with Polar Bears. In some locales, Wolves prey upon Polar Bear cubs, with one or more wolves harassing and distracting a mother bear while others attack and kill a cub.

SEAWEED ON THE MENU (BOTTOM)

While waiting for freeze-up, a Polar Bear on the shores of Hudson Bay munches on seaweed washed ashore from a previous storm. The seaweed offers little if any nutritional value, although rarely some crustaceans or fish may be consumed in the process. Seaweed may help fill an empty stomach during a fast that may last four or five months.

A WELCOME BOUNTY (TOP)

Photo: Adam Rheborg

Occasionally, a large whale dies and is washed ashore, providing a ready food source that may continue for a year or more. Bears will even dive underwater to grab hunks of meat, preserved somewhat in the cold Arctic waters. Normally solitary, Polar Bears may congregate peacefully at a large food source, and upward of twenty bears have been recorded at one time on a whale carcass.

FLOATING FOOD FEST (BOTTOM)

Photo: Adam Rheborg

Washed into the shallows of a bay in Svalbard, this Baleen Whale provides both a meal and a feeding platform. Frigid waters preserve the meat, which may provide meals in the ice-free summer for two years.

SMORGASBORD FOR ALL (TOP)

Photo: Hugh Rose/hughrosephotography.com
The remains of a Bowhead Whale on the shores of the Arctic Ocean provides a welcome feast for over a dozen Polar Bears. Native American Inuit kill a few whales each year, providing food for the community and leftovers for hungry bears. Bowheads are likely the longest-living mammal, reaching over 100 years of age.

ON THIN ICE (BOTTOM)

Photo: Hugh Rose/hughrosephotography.com
The first cold weather coats a quiet bay in ice that is still too thin to support the weight of an adult Polar Bear. This subadult tests the ice but is likely to return to solid ground until the growing cold makes the ice thick enough for easy walking.

AWAITING FREEZE-UP (TOP)

Photo: Steve Metildi

As winter nears, Hudson Bay begins to freeze and Polar Bears sense the change. Ice along the shoreline may form first, as the seas are calmer, but within days, the entire bay may be covered in a sheet of ice.

ONTO THE ICE (CENTER)

Photo: Steve Metildi

When I first visited Churchill, Manitoba, in the mid-1980s freeze-up occurred somewhere between the last week of October and the first week of November. Today, freeze-up of Hudson Bay occurs three weeks later, and the spring thaw, as ice disappears from the Bay, occurs earlier in the year. This has reduced the amount of time Polar Bears have to hunt seals, and this has resulted in a higher mortality of Polar Bear cubs, and in smaller litter sizes. This trend is likely not only to continue but to become worse.

THE BEARS' FUTURE HUNTING GROUNDS (BOTTOM)

Photo: Richard Day

A Polar Bear patrols a stretch of smooth fresh ice, watching for Ringed Seals that will be busy keeping breathing holes open as the first fast ice forms along the rocky shorelines.

ON THE ICE

The Polar Bear is sometimes referred to as the Ice Bear for a reason: its very existence depends upon the ice, for it is here that the bear finds most of its food. Ice in many areas is transitory, and only in the far north does pack ice remain year-round.

Some of the most productive hunting grounds for Polar Bears occur on the ice that forms through the winter along the shoreline and edges of glaciers and remains locked in place until the summer melt. This fast ice is often pocketed by the breathing and escape holes of Ringed Seals, and this is where Polar Bears will sit or lie in wait for hours, hoping that an unwary seal will surface for a breath.

Alarmingly, climate change is occurring most rapidly in the Arctic regions, as one event or reaction triggers another and reinforces the first, thus compounding the problem. For example, as the area of ice retreats further and further each year, more areas of dark, open water are exposed, and dark water absorbs sunlight, and thus heats up, rather than reflecting back into space. This melts more ice, opening up the seas and, if storms arise, generating bigger waves that in turn break up the pack ice even further. And so the cycle continues, reinforcing the effect and intensifying each year.

If sufficient food was available on land, Polar Bears would not be as dependent upon ice, just as the Polar Bear's ancestor, the Brown or Grizzly Bear, is not dependent upon ice today. But for the Polar Bear, it is here, in the ice, that the seals that comprise most of the bear's diet are found, and for this carnivorous bear, the ice is the key to survival.

CONSTANT WANDERINGS (LEFT)

Fresh tracks in soft ice mark the passage of a Polar Bear. Sometimes the trail meanders in a seemingly random manner, though it is likely that the bear is investigating new scents. Tracks in a straight line might indicate a male that had scented either a female or a fresh kill that the bear will try to scavenge.

CONSTANT TRAVEL (TOP)

Photo: Hugh Rose/hughrosephotography.com
Polar Bears travel constantly, and the average bear may cover the equivalent of a coast-to-coast trip across the United States in a single year. Bears may travel ten to twenty miles a day, but some bears may double that distance when necessary.

HUNTING THE EDGE (BOTTOM)

A Polar Bear follows the edge of the fast ice, perhaps heading toward an unbroken expanse of ice where Ringed Seals will maintain breathing holes. If necessary, bears will swim toward new locations, but they are more likely to remain dry if they can.

A LEAD (TOP)

While the Arctic seas may appear calm, tidal forces, currents, and wind are constantly at play, and sometimes the stress cracks and spreads the ice. These openings, called leads, may extend for miles, before the ice slides together again, often forming pressure ridges that resemble miniature mountains. This movement of the ice inspired the concept of continental drift, a theory once discounted but now universally accepted as an explanation for much of the planet's landforms.

A DAUNTING MAZE (BOTTOM)

Photo: Adam Rheborg

Polar Bears prefer platforms of solid ice, and head either to land or to pack ice once the ice cover drops to less than 50 percent of the total area. For this bear, any travel will involve a lot of swimming until the bear reaches a more stable platform. As the Arctic warms, more and more ice platforms shrink, making travel for the bear increasingly difficult.

TRAILING ALONG (TOP)

Photo: Adam Rheborg

A mother Polar Bear leads her two cubs across the fast ice that formed along a glacier's face. This is prime Ringed Seal habitat, and this family may remain in the general area, hunting seals, until spring arrives and the fast ice melts.

THE GLACIER FACE

(BOTTOM)

Photo: Adam Rheborg

A Polar Bear pauses on a small iceberg, calved from the towering glacier nearby. Glaciers, like this one in Svalbard, are retreating so rapidly that the shallow water nearby may be relatively unproductive, as the sea bottom has not yet responded to the change. With time, the now-exposed sea floor will support a variety of life.

A SPECTACULAR LOOKOUT (TOP)

Photo: Adam Rheborg

Rising high above the surrounding sea and often steeply walled, icebergs are not productive hunting areas for Polar Bears. Some icebergs are blue, an indication of old ice where gases have been forced from the ice over time. Analysis of the remaining air trapped within an iceberg or a glacier provide clues to the Earth's past climates.

PATIENTLY WAITING (BOTTOM)

Although this Polar Bear appears to be sleeping, it is actually on the alert. Should a seal surface for a breath of air, the bear will respond instantly, attempting to catch its prey before the seal can escape beneath the ice. Bears typically remain an hour or so at a breathing hole, motionless, as any movement might be detected by an approaching seal.

TOO MANY CHOICES (FOLLOWING PAGE)

Photo: Adam Rheborg

As ice begins to melt, Ringed Seals may surface anywhere. For a Polar Bear, a hunt becomes a game of chance. Ringed Seals may use the same breathing hole or lead several times, but will eventually move on to another, lessening the chance of it being ambushed. Eventually, there will be too many holes to choose from, and the bear must move on, either returning to land or moving off onto the pack ice.

> **"** . . . FOR THE BEARS, HUNTING BECAME EASIER, AS SEALS WOULD BE UNABLE TO SPOT A DISTANT, STALKING BEAR."

IN THE FOG (ABOVE)

As warm air passed over melting fast ice, a thick fog developed. From our ship, spotting distant Polar Bears became an almost impossible task, but for the bears, hunting became easier, as seals would be unable to spot a distant, stalking bear.

THE CHARGE (TOP)

Polar Bears travel at a steady pace of about two-and-a-half miles an hour, which they can maintain for days. Their powerful build is not designed for speed, but in a charge after a stalk that takes the bear within 100 yards of a seal, Polar Bears can reach twenty-five miles per hour, as it races to catch a seal before it can slip into the water and safety.

BLOODY FUR (BOTTOM)

Photo: Tom Wester

Swaths of blood soil the immaculate fur of a Polar Bear, evidence of a fresh kill. In spring, when Ringed Seals are giving birth and nursing young, and through the first weeks of summer, when weaned young seals are still naïve and vulnerable, Polar Bears may make a kill every three to five days. This is their time of bounty, as they put on the layer of fat they'll need to survive during the ice-free months.

STILL HUNTING (PREVIOUS PAGE)

Perhaps the lingering scent of a seal has prompted this Polar Bear to hunt along this ice edge. Polar Bears may lie still like this for hours, patiently waiting for a seal to surface for a breath. The energy expended by hunting in this way is minimal, but success is still a matter of some luck.

CATCHING THE SCENT (BELOW)

It is fairly certain that Polar Bears can detect prey or fresh kills from about one mile away. When a seal is seen, or smelled, the bear begins its stalk. Hunting in this way is less productive than still hunting (more on this on page 60), where a bear waits at a breathing hole—but watching a hunt transpire in this manner is certainly exciting!

THE HUNTER

Most bears are omnivores, eating both plants and animals, but the Polar Bear is the exception, as it is a true carnivore or meat-eating animal. Technically, the bear is an obligate predator, requiring meat in order to thrive. Polar Bears will consume berries, grasses, and seaweed, the latter perhaps just fulfilling an urge to fill its stomach, but the energy derived from vegetation plays almost no role in the bear's survival. Polar Bears eat meat, and when they can, they eat blubber, the stored fat of seals.

Seals are not easy prey. Much of their time is spent in the water, and when they are not, water is always close by. In most of the Polar Bear's range, Ringed and Bearded Seals comprise the majority of the Polar Bear's diet, and both seals have strategies to avoid predation. Ringed Seals usually stay within a yard or so of a breathing hole they keep open in the ice, allowing for a quick escape should they spot a bear. Bearded Seals climb up on ice floes, the smaller the better, so that they have an escape route handy from almost any direction.

For the Polar Bear, spring is the easiest time of year, as bears have the best chance of catching baby seals or nursing mothers. Some species of seals, like the abundant Ringed Seal, excavate dens in the snow that covers the fast ice where the seals have maintained their breathing holes. Polar Bears, should they catch the scent of a seal inside, will attempt to break through the roof of these snow caves before the seal or her baby can escape. Polar Bears succeed less than 10 percent of the time!

In spring, Polar Bears catch the majority of the food that will sustain them through the rest of the year, and in seal-rich areas, a bear may catch a seal every three days. If the bear is not lucky or skilled at hunting, weeks can pass before the bear either catches a seal or scavenges from the carcass left behind by a more successful bear. A fat, very proficient bear may eat only the blubber of a seal, ripping off the hide, inside out, and leaving the muscle and flesh of the seal untouched. These carcasses sustain hungry bears, especially subadults who need to hone their hunting skills.

By summer, the hunting becomes more difficult or even impossible in some regions. Then, bears either scavenge the sea coasts for carrion like washed up whales, walruses, or seals, or they retreat to the pack ice in the north, if that is possible. When bears are not crashing into seal lairs, they hunt by remaining motionless beside a seal's breathing hole, a method called "still hunting," or they actively stalk a seal by crawling on their belly across the ice until they are close enough to charge in for the kill, or they approach their prey by swimming, typically submerging before they reach the seal. Then, in a final explosive lunge, the

bear launches onto an ice floe and, if lucky, catches the seal.

Polar Bears will eat any animal or animal part to survive, including carrion, eggs, and even other Polar Bears, as cannibalism does occur. Even whales are a part of their diet. Small whales, like Belugas or Narwhals, are snatched from small openings in huge expanses of ice, or they are captured when the whales are stranded in unexpected low tides. If found, the carcasses of huge Baleen Whales are also consumed. Perhaps the most challenging prey is the walrus, as their formidable, yard-long tusks can deliver a lethal strike to any Polar Bear.

TAKE-AWAY LUNCH (TOP)

Photo: Steve Metildi

Bears often move some distance from the site of their catch or kill before consuming their meal. Doing so lessens the chance that a larger Polar Bear may steal the kill from its owner. Large male Polar Bears are notorious for this, growing fat on the bounty of smaller bears, including females with cubs.

BACON ANYONE? (BOTTOM)

Photo: Steve Metildi

When hunting is good, a Polar Bear may consume only the fat-rich blubber of a seal, leaving the rest of the carcass alone. This valuable meat may then be scavenged by other bears, particularly subadults whose hunting skills are lacking, and by Arctic Foxes that follow bears onto the ice in the winter months.

SHARING DINNER (TOP)

Photo: Hugh Rose/hughrosephotography.com

Subadult Polar Bears recently separated from their mother may remain together for weeks or months. When food is plentiful, bears may feed side-by-side amicably, but the dominant cub will hog any meal during lean times.

RESTAURANT WITH A VIEW (BOTTOM)

Photo: Adam Rheborg

An adult Polar Bear feeds on a seal on one of the many ice floes scattered at the base of a large glacier. Calving glaciers provide plenty of resting spots for seals, and good cover for the bears that stalk them.

THIS KILL IS MINE (TOP)

Photo: Adam Rheborg

While an adult Polar Bear feeds, a subdominant bear looks on from a distance. It is quite possible that the latter bear had made the kill but was driven off, usually without a fight. By patiently waiting for the larger bear to finish, a subdominant Polar Bear may still enjoy some leftovers.

STEALING A CATCH (BOTTOM)

Photo: Adam Rheborg

In the low light of an Arctic evening, a larger bear approaches a bear that had recently captured a seal. Bears of equal size may fight over a kill, although these altercations usually only involve posturing and teeth gnashing, and rarely physical contact. In a real fight, any injury incurred could ultimately prove fatal to either bear in an environment where one lives on a razor's edge.

A MEAGER SNACK (TOP)

Young and baby seals provide little nourishment, as their bodies still lack the energy-rich layer of blubber the bears relish, and are often left unconsumed. The meat does not go to waste, however, as Glaucous and Ivory Gulls, Arctic Foxes, and hungry bears will scavenge the remains.

RINGED SEAL (BOTTOM)

The favorite prey of the Polar Bear, Ringed Seals, when hauled out on ice, are constantly on the alert and usually within a seal's length of an escape hole. At the first hint of danger, the seal will slip into the hole and escape . . . unless the bear is faster!

LUCKY CATCH (TOP)

Photo: Richard Day

Until Hudson Bay freezes, Ringed Seals spend nearly all of their time in the water where they are safe from bears. This Polar Bear was lucky, capturing a Ringed Seal that swam too close to shore.

HUNTING PRACTICE

(BOTTOM)

Photo: Hugh Rose/hughrose photography.com

A Polar Bear subadult practices the pouncing behavior it will use to crash into the den of a Ringed Seal. In spring, Ringed Seals hollow out a birthing den beneath the snow, creating a subnivean igloo. Bears, smelling a seal inside, will pounce onto the roof of these dens, hoping to break through before the seal escapes.

THE HUNT

Photo series: Sue Altenburg

A Polar Bear pauses, smelling a concealed Ringed Seal in a den on an ice floe (**1**). With little warning, the bear leaps and crashes onto the roof of the den (**2**). The roof of the seal's den remains intact (**3**). The bear makes a second effort to break into the den but the roof holds (**4**). The Bear reaches into the den at the water line before the seal could make its escape (**5**).

The mother bear extracts the Ringed Seal from its den while her cubs, who sat waiting quietly nearby, rush in (6). Typical of many kills, the Polar Bear carried her catch far away from the site of capture with her cubs in hot pursuit. This behavior may lessen the chance that the seal might slither back into an escape hole—certainly not the case here (7).

6

7

HARP SEAL (TOP)

One of the most common of the sub-Arctic Seals, the Harp Seal is so-named because of the black lyre-shaped marking on the adult's coat. Baby Harp Seals, like the Ringed Seal, are born white, but unlike the Ringed, babies are born right on the ice. Polar Bears occasionally devastate large Harp Seal nurseries, although this seal usually gives birth far out to sea.

SEA STEALTH (CENTER)

Photo: Adam Rheborg

Polar Bears hunt either by still hunting or by stalking. Stalks may begin hundreds of yards away, with the bear slowly moving forward, freezing motionless whenever a seal looks up, and using ice floes and ridges as cover as it approaches.

FINAL APPROACH (BOTTOM)

Photo: Hugh Rose/hughrosephotography.com

Some of the most exciting hunts occur when a Polar Bear approaches a seal from the water. Bears will swim under ice floes to approach unseen, then, in the final instant, rocket out of the water, surprising the seal before it can escape. Less than half the time, a bear succeeds.

BEARDED SEAL (TOP LEFT)

Bearded Seals are the second most common prey item in most Polar Bear populations, but a large adult seal may weigh over 800 pounds, a very challenging catch for many female and most subadult Polar Bears. These seals feed on the mucky bottom of the sea floor, and iron oxides often stain their face and body an orange-red.

THE MUSTACHE SEAL (TOP RIGHT)

The prominent whiskers, or vibrissae, make identification of a Bearded Seal easy. The whiskers are on the muzzle, not the chin, so a more accurate name for this large seal would be Mustache, not Bearded, Seal.

PICKY EATER (BOTTOM)

Photo: Adam Rheborg

Polar Bears that enjoy a series of successful hunts become picky eaters, stripping the blubber from a seal carcass and leaving the rest behind. Fat provides far more energy than the protein-rich muscle, and given the chance, bears fill up their bellies with the most efficient food source.

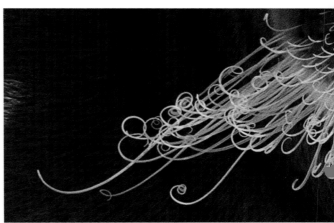

A CLOSE CALL (TOP LEFT)

The shredded rear flippers of this Bearded Seal are stark evidence of a previous encounter with a Polar Bear. These large seals are powerful animals, and by spinning and twisting, they may break the lethal grip of the bear and escape.

HARBOR SEAL (TOP RIGHT)

The seals are divided into two distinctive groups. Eared Seals include the Sea Lions and Fur Seals, which are not regularly found in the Polar Bear's range. Earless Seals, also known as True Seals, include all the species found within the Polar Bear's habitat, and include the Ringed, Bearded, and Harp Seal, among many others.

MAROONED (BOTTOM)

Photo: Adam Rheborg

When summer arrives, Polar Bears in the southern part of their range must come to land, where food is scarce. Hungry bears may go months without food, though in inhabited areas, Polar Bears may raid cabins or dumps as they seek food.

STALKING
THE BEACHES (TOP)

Photo: Hugh Rose/hughrose
photography.com

Bears may travel miles each day, searching the beaches for carrion. Dead seals, walruses, or whales occasionally wash ashore, and, if found, might sustain a bear or several bears for months.

POLAR BEAR &
WALRUSES (BOTTOM)

Photo: Adam Rheborg

A bull walrus may weigh over 3,500 pounds and is too large for all but the largest male Polar Bear to attempt to tackle. Still, a big walrus is a tempting target for a hungry bear.

TESTING (TOP)

Photo: Adam Rheborg

This Polar Bear stretches its neck out cautiously as it investigates a walrus herd that seems unconcerned by the bear's presence. Protected by other members nearby, walruses may hold their ground, secure in their numbers.

TRIGGERING PANIC (CENTER)

Photo: Adam Rheborg

Bears do kill walruses on occasion, and any given herd might panic when harassed by a bear. During the walruses' rush to the sea, calves may be killed or injured, and a bear will snatch any young walrus it can.

A FORMIDABLE WALL (BOTTOM)

Photo: Adam Rheborg

This walrus herd lumbered into the sea for safety, where they could now present a deadly formation of gleaming tusks. Once in the water, the advantage lies with the walrus, and Polar Bears have been killed when they unwisely proceeded with an attack.

PLAYING WITH THEIR FOOD (TOP)

Photo: Hugh Rose/hughrosephotography.com
A subadult Polar Bear plays with a walrus flipper that may have been from a scavenged carcass. The thick, meatless hide of this flipper offers little nourishment for a hungry bear.

DEADLY TUSKS (BOTTOM)

A male walrus's tusks, which may reach one meter in length, are deadly defensive weapons when directed at an attacking Polar Bear. A stab may result in a crippling injury that may eventually kill the bear, if the original wound alone isn't fatal.

BALEEN BANQUET (TOP)

Photo: Hugh Rose/hughrose photography.com

The carcass of a Bowhead Whale may sustain dozens of Polar Bears throughout the summer. Some whales die naturally and wash up onto beaches, while this one, in northern Alaska, was killed by Inuit in a traditional hunt.

CHOPPED STEAKS (BOTTOM)

Photo: Hugh Rose/hughrose photography.com

Ulu knives created the sharp edges on these slabs of meat and blubber from this Bowhead Whale. Whatever meat that is not used by the Inuit will be scavenged by the bears.

SHARING (FOLLOWING PAGE)

Photo: Hugh Rose/hughrose photography.com

Large numbers of Polar Bears may feed relatively amiably at a whale carcass, but such a bounty of food also attracts other scavengers, including wolves and Arctic Foxes. On Alaska's northern coast, dead whales also attract Grizzly Bears. This aggressive species will not only displace Polar Bears from a carcass, but in a few recorded cases, Grizzlies have also mated with Polar Bears to create a hybrid called the Prizzly or Grolar Bear.

MOTHERS & CUBS

For anyone who loves Polar Bears, seeing a mother bear and her cubs is a very special and endearing treat. Polar Bear cubs are undeniably cute, and little ones, struggling to keep up with mom as she strides across a snow field or weaves around pools of frigid water on a melting ice sheet, can tug at your heart. For the mother bear, parenthood is a daunting challenge, as the bear must not only find food for herself and her growing young, but must also remain vigilant for a male bear that might kill her cubs which would, in time, free her to mate with a male much sooner than the average two-and-a-half-year span involved in her raising cubs.

Pregnant Polar Bears face the greatest challenges. In some portions of their range, a female may have nothing to eat from the time the sea ice melts and deposits her on land, as early as late June in some locales, until she emerges from her den and returns to the winter sea ice in mid-March. That may entail a fast of as long as eight months. In order to survive that period, when she has to have enough stored fat to produce milk and nurture new cubs, she must put on hundreds of pounds of fat beforehand. Females normally stay with their cubs until they are approximately two-and-a-half years old, and at least during their second year together the nearly adult-size cubs can contribute to the family's success by occasionally catching a seal.

In the spring of the cubs' third year, their mother or a male who attempts to court her drives off her cubs, which may remain together for months before they separate to hunt the ice alone. Should the female successfully mate, her fertilized egg will not implant itself into the uterus lining until October or November, when development resumes. This delayed implantation and subsequent development of the fertilized egg results in the birth of a one- to one-and-a-half-pound cub sixty days later, in the dead of winter. The cub is tiny compared to the size of its mother and very undeveloped. However, by the time the cub and its mother emerge from the den, the cub will be large enough, at twenty to thirty-five pounds, to follow their mother to the sea ice. For a male cub, entering the ice for the first time may be the very last time he ever sets foot on land. For the next two years, he and his mother may hunt the pack ice, and he may continue to do so throughout his life.

ON THE ALERT (ABOVE)

A mother Polar Bear stands alert and on the lookout for any bear that might be attracted by the smell of blood. A male Polar Bear might not only steal her hard-won meal, but also kill her cub.

MESSY EATER (TOP)

Although this cub is only five or six months old, it is already eating meat. Cubs may remain with their mother for over two years, and may still nurse when they're nearly as large as their mother.

BUMP! (BOTTOM)

A mother bear pauses in mid-stride, causing a collision with her cub that was following behind. Cubs of the year, often termed COYs, almost always follow behind their mother, while cubs in their second or third year often travel ahead.

NEW MOTHER (ABOVE)

Photo: Katherine Pierce/CureUs Designs
Litter size varies, usually between one and three cubs. Bears with their first litters usually have one cub, as do older mothers who are nearing the end of their reproductive life. Single cubs, however, generally are larger and heavier than cubs that are twins or triplets.

> BEARS WITH THEIR FIRST LITTERS USUALLY HAVE ONE CUB,
> AS DO OLDER MOTHERS WHO ARE NEARING THE END
> OF THEIR REPRODUCTIVE LIFE."

TWINS (TOP)

Photo: Katherine Pierce/CureUs Designs

The average litter size of the Polar Bear is two. In litters composed of both sexes, male cubs grow faster than the females, and the size difference is obvious in only a few months. At two years of age, a male cub may be nearly as large as his mother.

TRIPLETS (BOTTOM)

Photo: Katherine Pierce/CureUs Designs

Mother Polar Bears in their prime may have three cubs, although it is likely that not all will survive. Prior to the 1990s, litters of triplets were not uncommon in western Hudson Bay, averaging about 12 percent of the cubs produced each year. This is no longer true, as climate change has shortened the seal-hunting season, resulting in pregnant females entering their dens weighing less than they did a few decades ago.

BIRTHING DEN (TOP)

Photo: Adam Rheborg

In Svalbard, Polar Bear mothers typically den in snowbanks on mountain slopes where the cubs are less likely to be threatened by wandering male bears. Male bears will kill cubs, freeing a female to mate again, as nursing mothers reject the advances of an amorous male.

A CHURCHILL DEN (CENTER)

Photo: Katherine Pierce/CureUs Designs

In Wapsuk National Park, Manitoba, Polar Bears often make their nursery dens thirty or more miles from the Hudson Bay, their hunting grounds. Here, bears excavate cave-like dens in the permafrost sometime during the fall. In winter, these dens are snow covered and well insulated.

DENNING UP (BOTTOM)

Photo: Richard Day

Polar Bears give birth in late December or January. In denning areas like Wapsuk, a mother bear may have fasted since mid-July, when the last ice melts in Hudson Bay. She will not eat until she leaves the den with her cubs, usually in March. For some bears, that is a fast of eight months!

WEIGHT LOSS (ABOVE)

Photo: Katherine Pierce/CureUs Designs
A mother bear may lose over 50 percent of her body weight between mid-July and March, when she leaves the den with her cubs, as she will fast the entire time she is denning. Cubs born to thin mothers may not survive, dying while still in the den or during the arduous march across the tundra to the sea where their mother will hunt once again.

WAIT FOR ME! (FOLLOWING PAGE)

Photo: Katherine Pierce/CureUs Designs
A mother bear and her cubs may remain several days around the birth den, giving the cubs time to strengthen muscles and become accustomed to the cold. Cubs may hitch a ride for a short time, but in their journey to the sea ice, cubs will travel under their own power. In Wapsuk, dens may be thirty miles from Hudson Bay.

> A MOTHER BEAR AND HER CUBS MAY REMAIN SEVERAL DAYS AROUND THE BIRTH DEN, GIVING THE CUBS TIME TO STRENGTHEN MUSCLES AND BECOME ACCUSTOMED TO THE COLD."

KEY TO SUCCESS (TOP)

Photo: Katherine Pierce/CureUs Designs

A fat, pregnant Polar Bear has the best chance of successfully raising her cubs through the first year of life. Pregnant females may gain as much as triple their body weight, giving the mother enough energy not only to give birth to as many as three cubs, but to successfully nurse the cubs for as long as three or four months before she has her first meal.

TINY BABIES (BOTTOM)

Polar Bear cubs average about one-and-a-half pounds at birth, perhaps the greatest difference in size between a newborn and an adult mammal. A large male Polar Bear may exceed 1,500 pounds—an increase of 1000 times over its birth weight!

DELAYED IMPLANTATION (TOP)

Polar Bears mate in spring, between late April and early June, but the active gestation period for the bear is only about two months long. After mating, the fertilized egg divides a few times and then stops until the bear enters her den when the egg, now known as a blastocyst, implants into the mother's uterus and continues to develop. This process is known as delayed implantation and occurs in seals as well.

VULNERABLE TO THE COLD (BOTTOM)

Photo: Katherine Pierce/ CureUs Designs

Young Polar Bear cubs are very vulnerable to the cold. The surface area of their body is great compared to their actual body mass, so heat can quickly radiate away, especially if a cub is wet. Adult bears, in contrast, have a much greater body mass in relation to their surface area, and consequently are less vulnerable to the cold.

THE LONG MARCH (TOP)

Photo: Katherine Pierce/CureUs Designs

In Wapsuk National Park, a mother and her cubs may travel for miles as she returns to Hudson Bay and the sea ice where she will resume hunting seals. Thin mothers produce thin cubs, and if her milk production is low, her cubs may die along the journey. Since the duration of the sea ice in Hudson Bay has shortened, pregnant females weigh less entering their dens in fall than they did thirty years ago. Litters of triplets are now quite uncommon.

HITCHING A RIDE (BOTTOM)

Photo: Katherine Pierce/CureUs Designs

Polar Bear cubs occasionally ride on their mother's back as she travels through the snow, but young cubs often do so when their mother swims through polar seas. Young cubs lack the insulation needed when immersed in frigid seas, and mothers avoid swimming when they can.

STAYING DRY (TOP)

Photo: Sue Altenburg

Two COYs try their best to stay dry as they follow their mother, hunting Ringed Seals across a landscape of ice floes. On a sunny day, a wet cub will dry off quickly by shaking its fur and rubbing against the snow.

FIRST SWIMS (BOTTOM)

Photo: Hugh Rose/hughrosephotography.com

By late summer, the polar seas are as warm as they'll ever be and COYs are big enough to tolerate the cold, either to play or to follow their mother if she swims among ice floes. With the expanse of polar ice shrinking each year, there is more danger of big waves developing in the open water when storms develop—a condition cubs cannot survive.

PLAY TIME (TOP AND BOTTOM)

Photos: Hugh Rose/hughrosephotography.com
Bears seem to be naturally playful, and this is most evident when a mother bear and cub take to the water. Older cubs may spend hours in shallow water, wrestling with one another or their mother, at least while her patience lasts.

DANGEROUS JOURNEY (TOP)

A mother bear marooned on land in Svalbard faces the possibility of an enforced fast for months. If ice floes are nearby, she may hunt for Bearded Seals, swimming from floe to floe with her cub following behind. Swimming burns calories, both for the mother and her cub, that may be needed to sustain both until freeze-up in the fall when the bear can hunt for seals more effectively.

BARREN GROUND (BOTTOM)

A bear can survive the three months or so she is marooned on land before the ice returns, and a fat mother may be able to nurse her cub during this time as well. Adult bears can undergo a walking hibernation physiological state during which their metabolism slows, even though they are still moving about and nursing their cubs—provided she has enough stored fat and energy to nurse!

TRACKS (BELOW LEFT)

Converging Polar Bear tracks may indicate where a mother bear and her nearly full-grown cub reunited or perhaps where an amorous male caught the scent of a female he is now following. Bears can easily travel twenty miles in a day, measured as a straight line from one point to another, but may actually cover three times that distance as they meander through the ice, hunting seals.

FALL APPROACHES (TOP RIGHT)

Photo: Katherine Pierce/CureUs Designs
In Churchill, Manitoba, winter ice usually returns by mid-November. This mother's cubs are now nearly half her size and will remain with her throughout the next year.

PROTECTIVE EYES (BELOW RIGHT)

Photo: Richard Day
A mother Polar Bear must always remain vigilant. Not only will male bears kill cubs to provide themselves with mating opportunities, but they also will cannibalize other bears when food is scarce. Adult females will attempt to intimidate threatening males, giving her young time to run off to safety, only to return after the danger departs.

NURSING (FOLLOWING PAGE)

Photo: Hugh Rose/hughrosephotography.com
This mother Polar Bear nurses her young on the flat fast ice on the northern coast of Alaska. Bears may nurse either by sitting down like this female, or by lying down on her back. Female Polar Bears have four nipples, giving the average litter of two cubs two teats to nurse from.

NURSING BED (TOP)

A mother Polar Bear may excavate a depression in a snow bank to make a comfortable back rest for herself while she nurses. A single cub, like this one, has a greater chance of survival, as the cub has access to all of its mother's milk. Single cubs are typically larger than cubs of the same age from litters of two or three.

WHICH ONE IS MOM? (FOLLOWING PAGE)

Photos: Hugh Rose/hughrosephotography.com
A mother Polar Bear may nurse her cubs until she finally drives them away for a life of their own, usually when the cubs are two-and-a-half years old. Cubs may be as large as their mother, and only when these two nursed was it readily apparent which one was the mother.

CLOSE TIES (ABOVE)

Photo: Tom Wester

While the mother Polar Bear is likely to make most of the kills, her two-year-old cubs are now sufficiently schooled that they can hunt on their own, although with limited success. When the cubs are finally driven off, they will face their greatest challenge as they learn to provide for themselves. In areas where seals are common, these sub-adults may survive by scavenging the kills of large males that eat only the blubber of their seal kills and leave the rest behind.

SPRING HUNTING (TOP)

Photo: Tom Wester

This mother Polar Bear and cub hunt the pack ice in spring, searching for the nursery den of Ringed Seals. In spring, when hunting is easiest, survival is still a challenge, and a bear averages about one seal per every three days of hunting. Pups, surprised in their den, are the most frequently captured prey, but provide little nourishment for a mother and cub.

FALL HUNTING (BOTTOM)

Photo: Richard Day

Bears hunt the smooth and flat fast ice for Ringed Seals at their breathing holes, and by fall, cubs are disciplined enough to stay quiet and still, allowing their mother to ambush a seal should it surface. If the cubs move, either in play or simply from boredom, sounds will travel through the ice and alert the seal to the potential danger.

SHAKING DRY (TOP)

After a short swim, a mother Polar Bear shakes herself dry while her cub looks on.

PLAY DAY (CENTER)

Photo: Hugh Rose/hughrose photography.com

Well fed from a summer feasting on the remains of a butchered Bowhead Whale, this cub and mother have enough energy to play in the last days of summer before a new season of hunting.

LONG SHADOWS (BOTTOM)

Photo: Richard Day

As freeze-up occurs along the southwestern shore of Hudson Bay, a mother Polar Bear and her cub head out onto the ice. Located below the Arctic Circle, the sun still sets during the summer solstice and rises above the horizon during the dead of winter.

DISTINCT POPULATIONS (ABOVE)

Photo: Hugh Rose/hughrosephotography.com
A mother bear and her two-year-old cub head out onto the ice toward the Arctic Ocean. Polar Bear scientists have divided the world's Polar Bears into nineteen subpopulations, like the Barents Sea bears seen here. Most members stay within their own subpopulations, but some bears wander widely, covering thousands of miles in a year.

> POLAR BEAR SCIENTISTS HAVE DIVIDED THE WORLD'S POLAR BEARS INTO 19 SUBPOPULATIONS, LIKE THE BARENTS SEA BEARS SEEN HERE."

AT PLAY

Although the Polar Bear is considered a solitary species, one where only a mother and cubs or the temporary liaison of a mating couple relieve this lonely existence, Polar Bears can be both social and quite playful when conditions draw bears together. At whale carcasses, where a dozen or more Polar Bears may congregate to feed, bears do so amiably, secure perhaps in the knowledge that there is enough for all. In the vicinity of Churchill, Manitoba, Canada, where hundreds of Polar Bears gather or pass by as they await Hudson Bay's freeze-up, young male bears may spend hours playfully wrestling with one another. Cubs, either with each other or, sometimes, with their tolerant mother, spend much of their day at play, sometimes spoiling their mother's hunt for seals by doing so.

Play activity is common among predators, even such solitary creatures as the Polar Bear. In some, this playfulness is only exhibited during courtship, when normally staid creatures appear to act foolishly, perhaps liberating their souls, if I can call it that, in these moments of interaction. Sometimes the weather triggers playful behavior. I've seen full-grown male African Lions rear up on their hind legs, boxing with one another, their claws sheathed inside their paws and their deadly fangs purposefully hidden in a display of non-aggression, just after a soaking rainstorm. African Wild Dogs and Asiatic Dholes, or Indian Wild Dogs, foxes and coyotes, all will box and mouth and hop over one another in play, sometimes for minutes on end.

Herbivores play as well, and you'll witness this activity if you're in the field long enough. Young zebras and gnus, still amazed perhaps at the liberating abilities of their long legs, race in circles around their mothers or chase one another across the grasslands. Gray Squirrels in your backyard seem to play tag, chasing one another up and down tree trunks, and even birds play, as Swallows drop a feather and snatch it in mid-air repeatedly.

For the Polar Bear, play no doubt relieves the tedium of waiting for the ice to return and may also serve to help define a bear's status and strength within its population. A friendly bout will, nonetheless, provide clues as to each contestant's strength, establishing a dominance hierarchy that may forestall a more serious encounter later on. By the act of playing, Polar Bears may lessen the chance of injury through unnecessary contests over food or mates, when any wound could lessen a bear's ability to survive. Play, then, may not only be fun, it may be a great strategy for survival.

HARMLESS PLAY (TOP AND BOTTOM)

Photos: Tom Wester

In Churchill, Manitoba, subadult male Polar Bears frequently wrestle as the air chills and Hudson Bay's freeze-up becomes imminent. Some encounters, like this one, look downright playful, while others, to the untrained eye, appear to be serious fights.

ESTABLISHING DOMINANCE

Photo, above: Tom Wester
Photo, following page, top: Hugh Rose/
hughrosephotography.com

While most of the wrestling matches involve subadult males, adult males may engage in contests as well. Although this may be a form of play to relieve boredom, these matches also help to establish a pecking order where bears learn who is the strongest and most aggressive in situations that are not serious or life-threatening. Only rarely does a session get serious and injuries result.

GENTLE MOUTHS (TOP)

Photo: Richard Day

Carnivores at play, be that a wolf, African Lion, or Polar Bear, convey their harmless intentions by not revealing their sharp and dangerous canine teeth, or fangs. Typically, the animal's muzzle covers these fangs, lessening the chance of inflicting accidental injury.

PINNED! (CENTER)

Wrestling matches can go on for hours, often with one opponent on top for a few minutes, and then flat on his back the next. Matches that get rough are sometimes ended by a bear grabbing his opponent's neck and forcing submission. This technique is also employed in disputes over kills, triggering a submissive posture in the weaker bear. This behavior is seen in a variety of predators, including your family dog!

WATER GAMES (BOTTOM)

Photo: Hugh Rose/hughrosephotography.com

Two subadult Polar Bears played for hours in small pools formed in the developing fast ice. A layer of fat and a dense underfur two inches thick overlaid by thicker guard hairs that may be six inches long insulate these bears from the cold and wet.

SLIDES (TOP)

On the hill and mountain slopes in Svalbard, you might see long ribbons of disturbed snow where a Polar Bear slid on its belly downhill. Bears apparently do this for fun, as tracks sometimes lead back up the hill where the process is repeated.

IDLE THREAT (CENTER)

Photo: Tom Wester

While these two subadult Polar Bear males were just playing, their posture resembles that of two bears that might square off in a more serious altercation. In what is known as a displacement activity, bears will yawn, just as a bull moose may paw the ground. Bears may step sideways and rear up high, showing off their size in a further effort to intimidate their rival.

SYNCHRONIZED ROLLING (BOTTOM)

Photo: Hugh Rose/hughrosephotography.com

For several minutes, these two subadult bears, possibly siblings, rolled and stretched in near-perfect synchrony, much to the delight of the tourists photographing them nearby.

BEAR WATCHING & SCIENCE

Living in a remote landscape of snow and ice, Polar Bears offer the lure of exotic travel for the ecotourist and the challenge of conducting meaningful research for the Polar Bear scientist. Polar Bear tourism is big business in Churchill, Manitoba, Canada, a small town on the shores of Hudson Bay that bills itself the "Polar Bear capital of the world." Far above the Arctic Circle, Svalbard, Norway, hosts thousands of tourists each year who travel here each summer in the hopes of seeing Polar Bears and other Arctic wildlife. Tourism also plays an important role in small villages and towns along the coasts of the Arctic Ocean in northern Alaska, and to a limited extent in Canada and Greenland. Seeing a wild Polar Bear is a thrill, and I can certainly attest to the fact that the experience never gets old.

The science of studying Polar Bears is perhaps among the most challenging of tasks, considering the environment, the weather, and the vast distances involved. Today, some of this Polar Bear research is done remotely, using GPS collars that communicate data via satellites to scientists working in labs far removed from punishing Arctic conditions. Collared Polar Bears have provided valuable information on their movements, the distances they travel, their periods of activity, and more. However, some conservationists argue that on-site observations provide more meaningful data without the risk that collaring a bear entails.

Climate change poses an extremely serious threat to the long-term survival of the Polar Bear, although this species has survived past warming events between other interglacial periods. Today, however, Polar Bears facing a relatively ice-free future also must deal with fewer dead animals to scavenge from when on land, as the seas have been over-exploited for centuries and whales, seals, and walruses are less common today. Bears, on land, also face a threat they did not have in past climatic events—man. Hungry, land-bound Polar Bears visiting villages, camps, outposts, and commercial operations in their search for food, lured by smells of drying meat or fish or trash, may be met by guns. Although Polar Bears enjoy worldwide protection in theory, exceptions are made when human life is perceived to be threatened, and in significant portions of their range, Polar Bears are hunted legally and poached illegally in many others.

Sadly, some Polar Bear scientists argue that since climate change and the loss of ice poses such a serious problem, the "harvest" of bears through hunting, done to maintain traditional hunting rights of local Arctic people or to infuse revenue in their communities, is insignificant compared to the greater threat of a warming climate and the loss of the Arctic ice. Some concerned conservationists counter that the killing of any bear only intensifies the threat to the Polar Bear's long-term survival, especially when hunting quotas are often based on inconclusive data for the populations that are hunted.

As with so many of the world's top predators, animals like the African Lion, down to perhaps less than 20,000 animals from 100,000 just forty years ago, or the tiger, reduced to fewer than 3,000 throughout their once vast range, Polar Bears are in serious danger, assaulted seemingly from all sides by a host of threats. I know it is a sad way to end a book celebrating the life and beauty of the Polar Bear and its world, but perhaps, in our facing the reality of this threat, we can as a world community address these issues, and in doing so, actually save ourselves, too.

SECURE AT THE TOP (TOP)

Photo: Katherine Pierce/CureUs Designs
Large male Polar Bears have little to fear, either on the ice or when marooned on land during the summer months. Resting on the crest of a small hill, this Polar Bear waits for the return of winter's ice.

HEAVY WEIGHT (BOTTOM)

Photo: Steve Metildi
In Churchill, Manitoba, Polar Bears may be marooned on land for nearly five months, eating nothing during that time. To survive, bears slow down their metabolism and enter a walking hibernation state, much like what Black Bears and Grizzly Bears undergo during their winter hibernation. Bears do not hibernate as true hibernators do, when

their body temperature and heartbeat drop to death-like levels, but the bear's metabolism does slow down.

TUNDRA BEAR

(TOP AND BOTTOM)

Photo, top: Tom Wester
Photo, bottom: Katherine Pierce/CureUs Designs
Although Polar Bears are most closely associated with ice and snow, in the southernmost portion of their range around Hudson and James Bays, bears can be found among stunted willow and evergreen trees where they spend the ice-free summer months.

GETTING RESTLESS (TOP)

Photo: Steve Metildi

During the warmest months of summer, land-bound Polar Bears may do little more than sleep, although as the temperature drops, bears along the southern shores of Hudson Bay begin a journey to the north-west where the first ice will form.

CHECKING THE SHALLOWS (BOTTOM)

Belugas, a small, white, toothed whale, frequent the river mouths emptying into Hudson Bay, and occasionally falling tides trap one. Only ten or twelve feet long, a stranded Beluga is easy prey for a large bear.

cabins, and at one time frequented an open dump where they scavenged the garbage. Fortunately, that dump is now closed.

AN ECOTOURIST INDUSTRY (BOTTOM)

Two young male Polar Bears wrestle in play near a Tundra Buggy, a specially outfitted vehicle that transports thousands of tourists each year into the tundra outside of Churchill, Manitoba. As the world's climate has changed, travelers are occasionally disappointed to find the "ice" bear in a drab, gray-brown, snow-free landscape.

POTENTIAL TROUBLE (TOP)

Photo: Hugh Rose/hughrosephotography.com
Migrating northward, Polar Bears pass by close to the town of Churchill, Manitoba. Hungry bears occasionally break into

CURIOUS BEARS (TOP)

Photo: Richard Day

In many parts of their range, Polar Bears may never see a human being, although those they do see may pose a grave threat, as bears are hunted and poached. In Churchill, the bears are protected, and instead of running off at the first sign of man, they will investigate with curiosity the vehicles they see.

WATCH OUT! (BOTTOM)

Years ago, a photographer who was not paying attention had his arm bitten by a Polar Bear. That could have been me, for I had been photographing a bear while using a heavy sweater as a lens rest. Distracted for a moment, I looked down to find a Polar Bear had reared up and grabbed my sweater. I quickly grabbed the other end and began a tug-of-war, a battle I knew I'd lose. The bear took my sweater to the ground and played with it for a few minutes, and finding it inedible, walked away. The sweater could have been my arm!

CURIOSITY (TOP)

Photo: Tom Wester

While it is tempting to be so close to a bear, one must be cautious. An upward lunge, perhaps simply done playfully, could result in tragedy for anyone with a hand or arm draped over the edge of a vehicle.

BEAR TRAP (BOTTOM)

Photo: Steve Metildi

Polar Bears sometimes become pests around human habitation, raiding trash bins, breaking into cabins, and potentially endangering people's lives. This live trap in Churchill was set along the outskirts of town for a bear that had been causing concern.

THE BEAR JAIL (TOP)

Photo: Steve Metildi

Problem bears in Churchill are housed in "the bear jail," where they will remain until Hudson Bay freezes, although some bears may be helicoptered north and then released if the jail is full. Bears are not fed while in the jail, since in the wild, before freeze-up, they would not be eating, either. By not feeding jailed bears, bears are not trained or conditioned to come into town, go to jail, and get a free meal!

HELICOPTER RIDE

(BOTTOM)

Photo: Richard Day

Bears may be transported from a capture site, and are ferried off to a release location, via helicopters. This is expensive, but Churchill's program of jailing and transporting bears has worked, keeping bears and people safe.

AWAITING FREEZE-UP (TOP)

Photo: Richard Day

Tourists in Churchill come to see the bears. When I started going to Churchill in the late 1980s, Hudson Bay froze over sometime around the first week of November. Now, freeze-up occurs as late as mid-December, but every year is different. If freeze-up occurs early, the Polar Bears vanish as they head out onto the ice, leaving late-season tourists very disappointed.

AIRPORT BEAR (BOTTOM)

Tourists arriving at the luggage carousel in Svalbard, Norway, meet their first Polar Bear and hope that this one isn't the only bear that they will see. Most tourists are not disappointed, provided they are visiting at the right time and to the right areas. Not everyone does so.

SHIP-BOUND TOURISM (TOP)

Photo: Adam Rheborg
Svalbard, an island archipelago north of Norway and far above the Arctic Circle, is another hot spot for the ice-loving Polar Bear. Here, tourists view bears from the deck of ships or small inflatable crafts, called Zodiacs.

POTENTIAL STOW-AWAY (BOTTOM)

Although large cruise ships ply these waters on eco-tourism adventures, the best experiences are had on small ships. This Polar Bear approached our twelve-passenger ship out of curiosity, and by standing, could rest her paws upon the deck.

INTIMATE VIEWS (TOP)

Photo: Adam Rheborg

The author, Joe McDonald, photographing a Polar Bear from the deck of a small ship. With a canny and sensitive boat captain, tourists can obtain incredible images of bears and other wildlife. The trick is to let the curious bears come to you, and they usually do.

WHO'S INSIDE?

(BOTTOM)

Photo: Adam Rheborg

On a small ship, portholes are low enough for a curious bear to look inside. Imagine waking up in your bunk, looking outside, and seeing this!

ZODIAC CRUISING (TOP)

Little can compare to the thrill one gets being at ice or water-level with a Polar Bear, possible when doing a Zodiac cruise through the ice. Bears often approach the edge of the ice in curiosity, an extremely important behavior for a top predator living in such a harsh environment.

WARNING SIGN (BOTTOM)

Signs warn the residents and tourists in Svalbard that they are in bear country. Bears rarely enter town, but the chance of an encounter is always present.

Bear grazes on sedges and grasses or fishes for spawning salmon while fresh mammalian meat is a rarity in their diet. Being this close is too close, and with a Polar Bear, this might be suicidal.

HIKING IN SVALBARD (BOTTOM)

Tourists traveling on foot in the back country of Svalbard must be accompanied by an armed guide. Should a curious Polar Bear approach, guides will employ a variety of methods to discourage it, and only as a last resort may fire a rifle into the air or into the ground nearby. Bears are rarely killed, although the average is about two per year, and many conservationists believe bear spray or air horns might be a more prudent deterrent for a bear that approaches too close.

TOO CLOSE (TOP)

Brown Bears in some of the coastal national parks in Alaska are habituated to man, and sometimes tourists and bears get too close to one another. The omnivorous Brown

A CLOSE CALL? (TOP AND BOTTOM LEFT)

Photos: Hugh Rose/hughrosephotography.com

Who knows whether this Polar Bear wanted to play or wanted to eat, but this photographer on the northern coast of Alaska was not taking any chances. The photographer eventually slipped inside his vehicle, no doubt with his heart pounding loudly!

POLAR BEAR CURIO (TOP RIGHT)

Photo: Adam Rheborg

Polar Bears are protected in Svalbard, but hides and mounts can be sold here, imported from Canada where bears are still hunted. Many conservationists, concerned about the uncertain number of Polar Bears worldwide, worry that this commercialism further threatens an animal faced with extensive habitat loss from climate change.

RESEARCH (ABOVE)

Photo: Hugh Rose/hughrosephotography.com
Polar Bears can travel widely, and in the course of a year may walk the equivalent of crossing the United States from coast to coast. A bear with a GPS-equipped collar provides information on where a bear goes, how long it stays there, and, in some cases, how long it lives. Collars are designed to drop off after a year or so, but some bears are collared repeatedly.

"POLAR BEARS CAN TRAVEL WIDELY, AND IN THE COURSE OF A YEAR MAY WALK THE EQUIVALENT OF CROSSING THE UNITED STATES FROM COAST TO COAST."

COLLARING (TOP)

Photo: Adam Rheborg

The neck of a male Polar Bear is larger than his head, and any collar would eventually slip off. A female's neck is smaller, and these are the bears normally collared. The collars not only provide GPS information, but also allow scientists to find and follow bears, and to assess their condition and their breeding status. Concerned conservationists argue that less intrusive and more informative research could be done by direct observation, thus reducing the chances of injury or death that may occur by collaring bears.

CONTROVERSY (CENTER)

Photo: Hugh Rose/hughrosephotography.com

If the hunting is good, a Polar Bear can gain a tremendous amount of weight and mass. One collared female in Hudson Bay gained 684 pounds between November and July, and depending upon when a collar is attached such a weight gain could cause problems for the bear. In this cited example, the bear remained healthy and produced triplets when she denned that fall.

STINKER BEAR? (BOTTOM)

Photo: Adam Rheborg

Research can come at a cost. To collar a bear usually involves a chase from a helicopter, then a shot from a rifle firing a tranquilizer. Bears can be stressed, burning up calories they cannot afford to lose, or they can be separated from their cubs, although this is reported to be rare. Bears occasionally drown, too drowsy to save themselves. Conservationists point out that bears may break limbs or suffer internal damage during this process, or die sometime after handling. Some bears grow too big for their collars, and the area around the collar may get infected, creating a nasty condition referred to as "a stinker" by Polar Bear researchers.

their hunting skills in order to survive. Most Polar Bear scientists cite climate change and global warming as the bear's gravest threat, but many conservationists worry that hunting, only partially under a quota system, contributes significantly to the Polar Bear's plight.

HUNTING QUOTAS (BOTTOM)

Photo: Hugh Rose/hughrosephotography.com
Although the exact number of Polar Bears is unknown, with estimates ranging from 16,000 to 25,000, and even 31,000 by some, Canada and Greenland have a "harvest" quota. In Canada, where the greatest number of bears is legally hunted, Inuit, the native people of the Canadian Arctic, often sell their permits to hunters from the south. Although it is presently illegal to import any part of a Polar Bear into the United States, today, U.S., European, and Asian hunters buy these permits. With an unknown number of existing Polar Bears, concerned conservationists argue that the killing of any bear threatens the species' survival.

STARVATION (TOP)

Photo: Adam Rheborg
Young bears, when finally driven off by their mother or by an amorous male, must hone

GLOBAL WARMING (TOP)

Photo: Adam Rheborg

A lone Polar Bear sleeps on an iceberg. Currents may push this precarious perch far out to sea, where it may melt, with dire consequences for the bear. Polar Bears have successfully made swims of 100 miles, but a floating iceberg may disappear hundreds of miles from the nearest pack ice or island.

ON THIN ICE (BOTTOM)

Photo: Adam Rheborg

There is absolutely no question that global warming is a serious threat to the Polar Bear. Polar Bears evolved from the Grizzly Bear around 150,000 years ago or even longer, and since that time, the Earth has witnessed several periods of extensive cooling and warming. Today's warming temperatures are probably occurring faster than past climatic events, but bears did survive past warming trends.

WHAT ARE THE NUMBERS? (ABOVE)

Many Polar Bear scientists argue that a controlled "harvest," i.e., the killing of bears, is sustainable, but many conservationists argue that these harvest quotas are often based on estimates or guesses that are decades old, and actual bear numbers in quota areas are unknown.

❝ . . . MANY CONSERVATIONISTS ARGUE THAT THESE HARVEST QUOTAS ARE OFTEN BASED ON ESTIMATES OR GUESSES THAT ARE DECADES OLD . . . **❞**

COMPLETE PROTECTION? (TOP)

Since no one knows for sure how many Polar Bears exist, and everyone agrees that habitat loss due to climate change certainly threatens the bear, many concerned conservationist and laymen believe the bears should enjoy complete protection.

SOBERING FACTS

(BOTTOM)

As the planet warms, the Arctic has lost about 13 percent of its ice cover per decade since 1980, and has declined by more than 50 percent in three decades, decreasing in actual ice volume by 75 percent. Ice reflects light and heat, while now-exposed open sea water absorbs light and heat. Warmer waters generate greater waves and storms, which erode the pack ice, compounding the problem.

ADAPTABLE? (TOP)

Photo: Hugh Rose/hughrose photography.com

Sadly, in the short term, the Polar Bear as we know it may cease to exist, but Polar Bears did survive past warming trends and hopefully will do so again. I think everyone shares the hope that this iconic and magnificent animal continues to roam the Arctic.

WANDERING THE ICE

(BOTTOM)

This curious Polar Bear rested her paws on the deck of our ship before wandering off across the fast ice. To her, perhaps, the world has not changed, but it is likely she grows a bit hungrier every season, as ice melts earlier in spring and reforms later in the fall.

WHAT CAN WE DO?

(FOLLOWING PAGE)

Photo: Hugh Rose/hughrose photography.com

The threats to the Polar Bear are complex and may require radical thinking and changes, but it is perhaps most important to view the bear as that proverbial "canary in the coal mine," an animal that can serve as a warning beacon for us all.

INDEX

Murres, 38

Hubble Images from Space

The Hubble Space Telescope launched in 1990 and has recorded some of the most detailed images of space ever captured. *$24.95 list, 7x10, 128p, 180 color images, index, order no. 2162.*

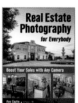

Real Estate Photography for Everybody

Whether you are a realtor or just want great photos of your home, Ron Castle shows you how. *$24.95 list, 7x10, 128p, 180 color images, index, order no. 2163.*

Art with an iPhone, *2nd ed.*

Kat Sloma's elegant images reveal the iPhone as a sophisticated art-making tool. In this book, she walks you through her inventive approach. *$24.95 list, 7x10, 128p, 300 color images, index, order no. 2165.*

Turning Heads
MODEL SHOOTS AND STORIES

Anthony Neste shares his best shots in the fashion and glamour genres— and some of the stories behind them. *$24.95 list, 7x10, 128p, 180 color images, index, order no. 2168.*

Top Dogs
PORTRAITS AND STORIES

Diane Costello shares stories about our constant companions and highlights the roles they play in our lives. *$19.95 list, 7x10, 128p, 180 color images, index, order no. 2162.*

Niagara Falls for Everybody
WHAT TO SEE AND ENJOY—A COMPLETE GUIDE

Make the most of your trip to Niagara Falls, NY, and Niagara Falls, CA, with this information-packed book. *$24.95 list, 7x10, 128p, 180 color images, index, order no. 2171.*

Big Cats in the Wild

Joe McDonald's book teaches you everything you want to know about the habits and habitats of the world's most powerful and majestic big cats. *$24.95 list, 7x10, 128p, 220 color images, index, order no. 2172.*

Cute Babies

Relax your mind and renew your sense of optimism by perusing this heartwarming collection of precious faces and tiny features. *$19.95 list, 7x10, 128p, 500 color images, index, order no. 2173.*

Bald Eagles in the Wild
A VISUAL ESSAY

Jeff Rich presents stunning images of America's national bird and teaches readers about its daily existence and habitat. *$24.95 list, 7x10, 128p, 250 color images, index, order no. 2175.*

Horses
PORTRAITS & STORIES

Shelley S. Paulson shares her love and knowledge of horses in this beautifully illustrated book. *$24.95 list, 7x10, 128p, 220 color images, index, order no. 2176.*